S0-BKO-354

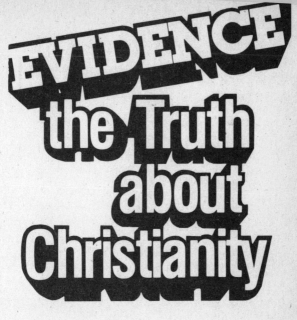

EVIDENCE
the Truth
about
Christianity

TERRY WINTER

HARVEST HOUSE PUBLISHERS
Eugene, Oregon 97402

Except where otherwise noted, all Bible verses quoted in this book are taken from THE HOLY BIBLE, NEW INTERNATIONAL VERSION Copyright © 1978 by New York International Bible Society. Used by permission.

EVIDENCE: THE TRUTH ABOUT CHRISTIANITY
formerly called WHY I AM A CHRISTIAN.

Copyright © 1979 by Harvest House Publishers, Eugene, Oregon 97402

Library of Congress Catalog Card Number: 79-87769
ISBN 0-89081-067-2

Contents

1

THE CREDIBILITY OF CHRISTIANITY TODAY

"Our world is so exceedingly rich in discussions that a truth is priceless."—Carl Justav Jung.

"When you cannot trust God, you cannot trust anyone, and when you cannot trust anything, you get the condition of the world as it is today."—Basil King.

Is Christianity true? That is the question of all questions. If it is true it demands our attention and beautifully meets our deepest needs. If it is false we ought to dismiss it altogether.

I am often asked to speak on the subject "The Credibility of Christianity Today." I am amazed at the interest in the subject and the attentiveness of the audiences. This obviously reflects a crisis of confidence in the subject in our contemporary world. There are so many confusing and contradictory voices heard on every side. There are so many claims to truth. What can we believe?

At the same time there has been a very deep erosion of confidence in the basic Christian message. I think this is in large part due to an ever widening communication gap. People today know little of the basic Christian claims and the evidence for their reliability and truth. Many are quite surprised to meet thoughtful people who are totally committed to a supposedly outdated, irrelevant, and probably faulty Christian gospel.

I can happily and positively say that there is overwhelming evidence to support the validity and credibility of the basic Christian message. I say this not only as a Christian communicator but as a searcher for truth myself. I am committed to finding truth and building my life upon it. I want to raise my family upon the truth. I want to live and relate to others in this world according to truth. I want to base my confidence in eternal life upon the truth. I, too, cannot settle for anything less.

FAITH

We talk a great deal about faith. But so often the word is used in such a vague and indefinite manner that it becomes a word that implies something less than certainty and confidence. It has become a blind leap into the dark. I am reminded of the little boy in Sunday school who was asked to define faith. His reply was "believing something you know isn't true." This is somewhat similar to the common use of the word hope. In the Bible it means a clear and certain promise that we look forward to. In everyday use it means we cross our fingers and wait to see what happens. Confidence has been replaced by a gamble of fate.

But Christian faith is so much more than a blind leap into the dark. It is a sure and confident step into the light. It is inextricably tied to the absolute trustworthiness of the Bible and of Jesus Christ. On one of our recent television programs I asked Earl Palmer, minister of the First Presbyterian Church in Berkeley, California, for a definition of faith. He used the word "trust" and said it means to put our weight down on the trustworthiness of the character and the claims of Jesus Christ. We can have confidence that Jesus Christ will be true to His word.

Webster's dictionary defines faith as "the assent of the mind to the truth of what is declared by another, firm and earnest belief on probable evidence of any kind." I still remember an excellent definition of faith given by one of my professors of theology, Dr. Edward John Carnell. He said, "Faith is the resting of the mind on the sufficiency of the evidence." Martin Luther long ago said "Faith is a living, daring confidence in God's grace. It is so sure and certain that a man could stake his life on it a thousand times."

Truth is all important in faith. We gather the evidence for the truthfulness of what we are considering and when it becomes sufficient we can confidently put our weight down, resting our minds, upon the dependability of this object of our faith. Christian faith is specifically considering the character and claims of Jesus Christ and when their reliability is established putting our weight down upon Him and believing in Him.

The claims of Christianity coincide with the deepest needs of our lives. Is this sheer coincidence or is it a hint that there is indeed a designer responsible for the design of our lives and the truth of Christianity?

THE LONGING WITHIN

Each of us has a longing for something more than we have experienced. We feel there is more to life than mere existence. This longing within is often expressed as a search—a search for happiness or genuine contentment, a search for meaning or lasting significance and a worthwhile life.

We all experience this inner longing for fulfillment. Is this hunger we share just an accidental aspect of human personality? Are we simply meaningless chemical and biological entities in a causeless and impersonal universe?

If indeed there is no God and the universe is merely a total of causeless events—molecular accidents—then where does our inner longing come from?

I am convinced that this longing indicates the existence of a personal and purposeful Creator who has placed within the heart of His creation a longing for harmony with Himself. He alone is both the Creator and Fulfillment of this longing for wholeness. Blaise Pascal, the eighteenth-century scientist and mathematician who wrote extensively about the Christian faith, spoke about a "God-shaped vacuum" within each of us that can only be filled by God Himself. Saint Augustine said, "Our hearts are restless until they find their rest in Thee."

Professor C.S. Lewis of Oxford University, a former agnostic, wrote a great deal about this longing within: "If within my heart I find a desire for something which nothing in this world can satisfy," he said, "the most probable explanation is that I was made for another world."

WHERE IS THE ANSWER?

A friend of mine told me he had never had an ultimate thought in his life until confronted with death during the Vietnam War. He had never really asked who he was, why he was here or what would happen when he died. He realized that he had no idea of what gave any significance to his life. When that thought hit him, he began to think about God. As a result he became a Christian.

I see no hope for wholeness or fulfillment without God—more specifically, without the God who has revealed Himself in the Bible and in Jesus Christ, the God of love and concern who is intimately involved in the affairs of our lives. I have read many statements despairing of the meaning of life *without* God that confirm Pascal's description of a vacuum.

Jean-Paul Sartre, the existentialist philosopher and

author of books and plays such as *No Exit*, has said, "Every existent [person] is born without reason, lives in weakness and dies by chance."

The American author Mark Twain had this to say about the struggles common to each of us:

> A myriad of men are born; they labor and struggle and sweat for bread; they squabble and scold and fight; they scramble for little mean advantages over each other. Age creeps up on them and infirmities follow; shame and humiliation bring down their pride and vanities. Those they love are taken from them, and the joy of life is turned to aching grief. The burden of pain, care, misery grows heavier year by year. At length ambition is dead; longing for relief is in its place. It comes at last—the only unpoisoned gift earth has for them—and they vanish from a world where they were of no consequence, where they achieved nothing, where they were a mistake and a failure and a foolishness, where they left no sign that they had ever existed—a world that will lament them a day and forget them forever.

Francis Schaeffer, one of the world's most incisive Christian thinkers, has analyzed the dilemma we face without God. "Man, made in the image of God, has a purpose to be in relationship to God, who is there. Man forgets his purpose and thus he forgets who he is and what life means."

Similarly, C.S. Lewis simply says "God cannot give us happiness and peace apart from himself, because it is not there. There is no such thing."

Is this how you see your own life?

On the other hand, I have read and listened to countless stories from people who found the answer to their inner longing when they became Christians and were born anew into a personal relationship of faith in Jesus Christ.

9

Charles Colson of Watergate notoriety wrote a bestselling book titled *Born Again,* in which he tells how his heart and life were turned around when he became a Christian.

C.S. Lewis, who became one of the most prolific and sharp-sighted contemporary writers on Christian faith, wrote this about his own conversion:

> You must picture me alone in that room at Magdalen, night after night, feeling whenever my mind lifted even for a second from my work, the steady, unrelenting approach of Him whom I so earnestly desired not to meet. That which I greatly feared had at last come upon me. In the trinity term of 1929 I gave in, and admitted that God was God, and knelt and prayed, perhaps that night, the most dejected and reluctant convert in all England.

Convinced by the truth of Christianity, Lewis felt he simply had to believe. His initial reluctance turned to joy and fulfillment when he discovered the answer to his longing within. In fact, he titled his autobiography *Surprised by Joy.*

MY OWN STORY

I seldom thought about ultimate questions, although I did wonder occasionally about the meaning of life. But I failed to connect it at all to what I knew about God.

As a child I had attended a boarding school where morning chapel attendance was required. Later I was confirmed in one of my hometown churches as a teenager. But any knowledge I had of Christianity totally missed the point about a personal relationship with God through faith in Jesus Christ.

In fact, I could not clearly define the word "Christian." I thought everyone in Canada was a Christian, some a little better and some a little worse, since we all lived in a Christian country.

When I was in my last year of high school I was invited to an evangelistic crusade. At first I wasn't interested and declined the invitation, but later my curiosity led me to change my mind and I agreed to attend.

I had never been to anything quite like it before. Everyone sang with enthusiasm and the atmosphere was warm and welcoming. The topic the speaker chose that night was his own story about how he had become a Christian believer.

I had never heard such a story. He explained how he came to realize his own sinfulness and his need of forgiveness, and how he recognized that Jesus Chirst's death on the Cross could provide that forgiveness. I understood what he was saying. I knew that I too was sinful and needed forgiveness, and I knew that somehow Jesus Christ was the answer.

After the evening program I was invited to a party where everyone talked and sang and had a good time. I had never seen such joy. These people had found a fullness and a peace that I lacked—what was it?

This was the beginning, or at least the next step, on a serious quest to find that "something more." For the next two months I attended church every Sunday—sometimes even three churches—and a youth group on Saturday.

One church I was attending had a special Christmas program. The Sunday school children were planning to stage a pageant followed by a special talk on the meaning of Christmas. As the speaker explained the meaning of Christmas, the concept of personally becoming a Christian suddenly dawned on me.

He spoke of God giving us Jesus Christ, and through Him forgiveness of sins and eternal life. But this gift, as all gifts, had to be received. What was I doing with the greatest gift of all?

11

I often use the example of a dimmer switch in a dining room to describe this moment. When I entered the auditorium for the pageant, the light was very dim. When I left, it was very bright. I do not recall any moment when I suddenly "saw the light." But I understood the dimension of personal faith in becoming a Christian. The truth of the Bible verse became clear: "For God so loved the world that He gave His only Son, that whoever believes in Him shall not perish but have eternal life" (John 3:16). This is the most well-known verse of the Bible, but I had never heard it before, or any other biblical quotation, for that matter.

The speaker asked those who wanted to become Christians to ask him for a booklet published by the Gideon Society and titled *The Way to Heaven*. I took the booklet home and read it. Then I knelt by my bed.

The prayer on the last page was titled *My Decision* and said, "Confessing to God that I am a sinner, and knowing that I stand to be condemned to everlasting hell, I now believe that Jesus Christ, God's Son, has paid my penalty by dying on the cross for my sins. I will trust Him henceforth as Savior and Lord of my life."

That was only the beginning. As Robert Frost, the poet, wrote, "Two roads diverged in a yellow wood . . . I took the one and that made all the difference." That new commitment, as simple as it was in the beginning, has made all the difference in my life.

Despite the difficulties, doubts and failures, I experienced the reality of the love of God and found a joy I had never imagined possible. I also found a sense of well-being and fulfillment in answer to my longing within that grows as I continue to grow as a Christian.

Today I can hardly remember what it was like not to have such a sense of purpose, meaning and significance in my life.

When I first became a Christian, my understanding of the content of Christianity was obviously limited even though my actual experience was fresh, strong and real. Now after 20 years of study, reflection and questioning every area of belief, my understanding of the gospel and my conviction of its validity has increased to the degree that I recommend it to everyone's open and sincere examination.

In the following chapters I talk about some of the main reasons why I am convinced that Christianity is the objective truth as well as the answer to what we seek in pursuing our longing within.

2

The Bible

"After reading the doctrines of Plato, Socrates or Aristotle, we feel the specific difference between their words and Christ's is the difference between an inquiry and a revelation."—Joseph Parker.

"If we are going to have answers for the twentieth century world, we must not only have a God who exists, but we must have a God who has spoken."—Francis A. Schaeffer.

The first major reason I am convinced that Christianity is true is because I am convinced that the Bible is the living Word of the living God. It is so profound and so relevant that I cannot dismiss it lightly. The Bible has the endorsement of some of the greatest scholars in the world. You could spend a lifetime studying it and never fully master it. Yet the Bible speaks to our lives, this moment, in an immediate, powerful and simple way.

When I consider the nature of the Bible, I see no other explanation for its existence than its own claim for itself—that it was inspired by God. If it were not, then we have something even more fantastic to explain.

Consider these facts:

The Bible was written over a 1600 year span;

By more than 40 authors separated over hundreds of years and miles:

Moses, a political leader in Egypt
Peter, a fisherman in Galilee
Paul, a well-educated rabbi
Luke, a medical doctor
Solomon, the wise king of Israel
Matthew, a converted tax collector
Amos, a fearless herdsman-prophet
David, the shepherd-king of Israel
Joshua, a great military general

Daniel, a prime minister in one of the ancient world's great civilizations;

In a wide range of locations:

wildernesses
prisons
hillsides
a palace;

On three continents:

Africa
Asia
Europe;

In three languages:

Hebrew
Aramaic
Greek;

In a variety of literary forms:

poetry
history
law
parable
biography
prophecy
personal memoirs
personal correspondence.

Yet in spite of such wide diversity, the Bible has a remarkable unity of theme and development of thought. The Bible is the story of God's revelation to men. It tells us who God is, who we are and what God's loving purposes are for us.

The Bible tells us how God can bring us back to Himself through the sacrifice of His Son and how we

16

can be forgiven and given the gift of God's life, which is eternal. The Bible then tells us how to live.

THE NECESSITY OF THE BIBLE

Without the Bible we would grope in the dark and search in vain for ultimate answers without ever finding them. We would be condemned to look for knowledge beyond ourselves; we could never rise above the limitations of our humanity.

That is why the Bible is properly defined as *revelation*. This is the name of the last book of the Bible, but it is also the nature of the whole book. The Bible is the revelation of God to man. It is God revealing Himself to us. It is our all-important guide.

If God had not spoken, we could never have found Him. If we are finite and He is infinite, then there is no possibility we could ever know Him and share His thoughts unless He first revealed Himself to us. He is beyond us because our sinfulness separates us from His perfect sinlessness.

Sometimes when we stand alone on a mountaintop we may feel "close to God." Watching a beautiful sunset, listening to great music or perhaps contemplating the complexities of life, we may feel an awe before the Creator and think that we share something of His wisdom and power.

But all these experiences fall short. They do not reveal the full character of God. They do not tell us about His love and sacrifice in Christ. They do not tell us about the nature of our sinfulness, our need to repent or the joy of knowing God. These are truths that must be revealed to us by God Himself.

The Bible is God specifically revealing to us what we could never know by ourselves. It is the revelation of

God's acts in history and their interpretations. The crucifixion and resurrection of Christ is central to understanding the revelation of God.

Before the coming of Christ, the Old Testament revealed the nature of God and the nature of man, and it prepared the way for the coming of the promised Savior. Then the New Testament recorded His life and teaching prior to His crucifixion, summing up the way in which we should live as believers in Christ. This practical side of the Bible should never be minimized. The wisdom that it gives us for living is unmatched by any other book.

WHY I BELIEVE THE BIBLE IS RELIABLE

I often hear people say, "If you could prove that the Bible is true, I would become a Christian." That is a fair statement. Frankly if I had not dealt with that question myself, I would not be a Christian today.

This essential question about the reliability or the truthfulness of the Bible raises several questions. Is the Bible reliable historically? That is, did the events happen exactly as they are recorded? And are the copies that we have today accurate copies of the originals?

Is the Bible authoritative in its claims? In other words, is it inspired? Is the Bible really the Word of God?

Has God indeed spoken? That is the ultimate question!

Before we proceed any further, let us stop and think about evidence. Here are some of the evidences that confirm the reliability of the Bible.

THE AMAZING NATURE OF THE BIBLE

I mentioned the amazing nature of the Bible. It is a

book written by a diverse group of people during hundreds of years, yet it demonstrates a remarkable unity. It is so deep and profound that the greatest minds are humbled by it; yet it is so simple and basic that even a child can understand it and come to know God. The Bible is surprisingly up-to-date in describing our civilization today, even though it was completed in a culture far removed from our own.

I once asked Dr. Ward Gasque, a friend of mine and a professor of New Testament at Regent College in Vancouver, why he believed the Bible is the reliable Word of God. He surprised me by his answer. Before listing all the academic reasons, he said simply that the Bible spoke to him as he read it. It addressed him where he was; he recognized in this that the Bible is not just an ordinary book, but the living Word of the living God.

THE BIBLE'S CLAIM FOR ITSELF

Unless we have reason to think otherwise, we usually allow someone else's statements to stand as primary evidence in making our own judgments. It is important to note that the Bible claims inspiration for itself. It repeatedly records such phrases as "the Word of God came to me, saying," "and God said" and "thus says the Lord."

One well-known quotation from the New Testament claims its own inspiration. "All Scripture is God-breathed and is useful for teaching, rebuking correction and training in righteousness" (2 Timothy 3:16).

How God inspired the various writers is a difficult question that we cannot fully answer. God certainly used the writers as more than dictating machines or secretaries. We can imagine that He led and directed and formed thoughts in their minds as they wrote. John was an uneducated fisherman who wrote simply, and Paul was a rabbi gifted with great learning. Yet both wrote under the inspiration of God, and their writings are part of our inspired Scriptures.

CHRIST AND THE BIBLE

Christ's own attitude toward the Bible is very important. If He truly was the Son of God, then His perspective on the Old Testament Scriptures would be God's perspective.

Christ was well-versed in the Old Testament, which was regarded by the people at that time as the only "Word of God." Often Christ would say "as it is written," and would speak with authority when quoting the Old Testament.

When tempted in the wilderness, Christ said, "It is written, man does not live on bread alone, but on every word that comes from the mouth of God" (Matthew 4:4). He plainly referred to an Old Testament quotation (Deuteronomy 8:3) as well as to the content of that quotation; the word that comes from God is an all-important reality.

Christ also said regarding "the law and the prophets" (the Old Testament Scriptures), "Do not think that I have come to abolish the Law or the Prophets; I have not come to abolish them but to fulfill them. I tell you the truth, until heaven and earth disappear, not the smallest letter, not the least stroke of pen, will by any means disappear from the law until everything is accomplished" (Matthew 5:17, 18). Jesus taught that every thought, sentence and word in the Old Testament came from God.

THE EARLY CHRISTIANS AND THE BIBLE

At the time Jesus quoted from the Old Testament, the early Christians had the Old Testament and the beginnings of the New Testament. The teachings of Jesus and His disciples were passed on orally from person to person until they were recorded in written form.

From the beginning these oral teachings were just as important as those of the Old Testament. Careful attention was given to the accurate communication of the teachings. Their memorization became the basis for their faith and their lives.

Saint Paul, who wrote much of the New Testament regarded both the Old Testament and the New Testament as God's good news. "Now, brothers, I want to remind you of the gospel I preached to you, which you received and on which you have taken your stand. By this gospel you are saved, if you hold firmly to the word I preached to you. Otherwise you have believed in vain. For what I received I passed on to you as of first importance: That Christ died for our sins according to the Scriptures, that He was buried, that He was raised on the third day according to the Scriptures" (1 Corinthians 15:1-4).

The early Christians were those who had listened to the teachings of Jesus and His disciples. As the spoken teachings and then the writings took place, they were the best witnesses to judge that these developing traditions were the reliable Word of God.

SCHOLARS AND THE BIBLE

If the scholars today who study ancient documents were to make skeptical judgments about the reliability of the Bible, my confidence would be badly shaken. But just the opposite is the case.

What do they say?

Howard Vos, who wrote *Can I Trust the Bible?*, said:

> From the standpoint of literary evidence, the only logical conclusion is that the case for the reliability of the New Testament is infinitely stronger than for any other record of antiquity.

Noting that there are over 5000 Greek manuscripts of the New Testament, Sir Frederick Kenyon, a scholar of New Testament criticism, says this regarding the reliability of our current texts in his *Study of the Bible:*

> It cannot be too strongly asserted that in substance the text of the Bible is certain: Especially is this the case with the New Testament. The number of manuscripts of the New Testament, of early translations from it, and of quotations from it in the oldest writers of the church is so large that it is practically certain that the true reading of every doubtful passage is preserved in some one or other of these ancient authorities. This can be said of no other ancient book in the world.

The same author in *The Bible and Archaeology* says this about the text of the Bible:

> The interval then between the dates of the original composition and the earliest extant evidence becomes so small as to be in fact negligible, and the last foundation for any doubt that the Scriptures have come down to us substantially as they were written has now been removed. But the authenticity and the general integrity of the books of the New Testament may be regarded as finally established.

In recent years the discovery of the Dead Sea Scrolls has created a sensation among Bible scholars and has given further evidence about the reliability of Scripture.

These 40,000 inscribed fragments were found in 1947 stored in clay jars and deposited in hillside caves overlooking the Dead Sea. They are scrolls and copies of the Old Testament used by people in the Qumran community living at the time of Jesus. By comparing these manuscripts to the oldest we had before their discovery (dating from 900 A.D.), we can support the reliability of the Old Testament.

Gleason Archer, an Old Testament theologian, says that the copies of the book of Isaiah found in these scrolls "proved to be word-for-word identical with our standard Hebrew Bible in more than 95 percent of the text. The 5 percent variation consisted chiefly of obvious slips of the pen and variations in spelling."

Millar Burrows, writing in *The Dead Sea Scrolls,* concludes, "It is a matter of wonder that through something like a thousand years the Text underwent so little alteration."

What do scholars say about the authenticity of the original biblical records, which is the other part of question on reliability?

F.F. Bruce, professor of Biblical Criticism at Manchester University, says:

> *The earliest preachers of the gospel knew the value of firsthand testimony, and appealed to it time and again. "We are witnesses of these things," was their constant and confident assertion. And it can have been by no means so easy as some writers seem to think to invent words and deeds of Jesus in those early years when so many of His disciples were about who could remember what had and had not happened.*

23

He continues with this interesting observation:

> And it was not only friendly eyewitnesses that
> the early preachers had to reckon with; there
> were others less well disposed who were also
> conversant with the main facts of the ministry
> and death of Jesus. The disciples could not af-
> ford to risk inaccuracies (not to speak of wilful
> manipulation of the facts), which would at once
> be exposed by those who would be only too
> glad to do so.

ARCHEOLOGISTS AND THE BIBLE

Archeology, an important science in reconstructing
history and learning about past civilizations and
cultures, also supports the reliability of the Bible.

Burrows of Yale University writes, "On the whole,
. . . archeological work has unquestionably strengthened confidence on the reliability of the scriptural
record. More than one archeologist has found his
respect for the Bible increased by the experience of ex-
cavation in Palestine."

William F. Albright of Harvard University said,
"There can be no doubt that archeology has confirmed
the substantial historicity of the Old Testament
tradition."

Nelson Glueck, a well-known Jewish archeologist,
said, "It may be stated categorically that no archeological discovery has ever controverted a biblical
reference."

These scholars confirm that both the Old and New
Testaments are accredited by archeological evidence.
Recent discoveries continue to confirm the reliability of
the Bible.

One example concerns the details which Luke

24

recorded about the birth of Jesus. Critics had said that there was no census, that Quirinius was not the governor of Syria at that time, and that everyone did not have to return to his ancestral home as Joseph did.

But recent archeological discoveries have shown that there was a regular census every 14 years. An inscription found in Antioch reveals that Quirinius was indeed the governor of Syria at that time. And a papyrus document found in Egypt gives directions for the taking of a census that included details of Jews returning to their ancestral homes.

Sir Frederick Kenyon concludes, "Archeology has not yet said its last word; but the results already achieved confirm what faith would suggest, that the Bible can do nothing but gain from an increase of knowledge."

The Bible has been respected for years, but it deserves more than our respect. We should read it and allow it to speak to our lives today. It is a book that understands our hearts and can give us the knowledge we so desperately need to personally know God in our lives.

> The word of God is living and active. Sharper than any double-edged sword; it penetrates even to dividing soul and spirit, joints and marrow; it judges the thoughts and attitudes of the heart (Hebrews 4:12).

3
Jesus of Nazareth

"I have a great need for Christ. Thankfully I have a great Christ for my need."
Charles Spurgeon.

"After six years given to the impartial investigation of Christianity as to its truth or falsity, I have come to the deliberate conclusion that Jesus Christ is the Messiah of the Jews, the Saviour of the world, and my personal Saviour."—Lew Wallace, Author of Ben Hur

"It is on the unshakable fact of the resurrection of Christ from the dead that I base my faith in God's utter integrity and faithfulness. He let Jesus die—but only because he would raise him again. You can count on him! You can stake your faith on God—the God of Jesus Christ. He will keep his word."
—Leighton Ford.

The second major reason I am a Christian is because of Jesus Christ. Christianity rises and falls on Him. If He was all that He said He was, and if He did all the Bible claims that He did, we have all the evidence that we could ever ask for. And if Christ was not all these things, we have nothing. That is how important Jesus Christ is to Christianity.

This is the point at which my confidence and faith in Christianity is increasingly sharpened: I find Jesus Christ believable. If any man who has ever lived commands and deserves our respect and our commitment, it is Jesus Christ. I see in Him a man who is unique in all of history.

THE INCOMPARABLE CHRIST

More than nineteen hundred years ago there was a Man born contrary to the laws of life. This Man lived in poverty and was reared in obscurity. He did not travel extensively. Only once did He cross the boundary of the country in which He lived; that was during His exile in childhood. He possessed neither wealth nor influence. His relatives were inconspicuous and had neither training nor formal education. In infancy He startled a king; in childhood He puzzled doctors; in manhood He ruled the course of nature, walked upon the billows as if pavements, and hushed the sea to sleep. He healed the multitudes without medicine and made no charge for His service. He never wrote a book, yet all the libraries of the country could not hold the books that have been written about Him. He never wrote a song, and yet He has furnished the theme for songs. He never founded a college, but all the schools put together cannot boast of having as many students. He never marshalled an army, nor drafted a soldier, nor fired a gun; and yet no leader ever had more volunteers who have, under his orders, gone throughout the world to increase his kingdom. He never practiced medicine, and yet He has healed more broken hearts. The names of past proud statesmen of Greece and Rome have come and gone. The names of the past scientists, philosophers, and theologians have come and gone, but the name of this Man lives more and more. Though time has spread nineteen hundred years between the people of this generation and the scene of His crucifixion, yet He still lives. Herod could not destroy Him, and the grave could not hold Him. He stands forth upon the highest glory, proclaimed of God, acknowledged by angels, adored by saints, and feared by devils as the living, personal Christ, our Lord and Savior.

Anonymous

CHRIST'S CLAIMS ABOUT HIMSELF

Jesus made astounding claims. He claimed to be God. He said He could forgive sins. He promised eternal life to those who would follow Him.

We all make ourselves vulnerable when we make claims about ourselves. The greater the statements, the greater our vulnerability. We can be deeply respected if our claims are proven true, but we can be tragically rejected if our claims are proven false.

Jesus made so many claims that it is impossible to discuss them all. I think it would be most helpful if we studied the "I Am" passages from the Gospel of John.

> I am the bread of life. He who comes to me will never go hungry, and he who believes in me will never be thirsty (John 6:35).

Since bread is the source and sustenance of life, Jesus identifies Himself with life, and promises a quality of life that is total and complete.

> I am the light of the world. Whoever follows me will never walk in darkness, but will have the light of life (John 8:12).

Jesus here identifies Himself with light in the same sense of truth and insight into reality. While the world is dark and confused, Jesus gives us the light that brings meaning and reality to life.

> I am the gate of the sheep . . . I am the gate: whoever enters through me will be saved. He will come in and go out and find pasture. The thief comes only to steal and kill and destroy. I have come that they may have life, and have it to the full (John 10:7-10).

The proper entrance into a sheepfold was through a gate. Likewise, the true entrance to God is through a gate; Jesus is that gate.

> I am the resurrection and the life. He who believes in me will live, even though he dies; and whoever lives and believes in me will never die (John 11:25).

Here Jesus states that He is Lord over death. He will rise again, and so will those who believe in Him.

> I am the way, the truth, and the life. No one comes to the Father except through me (John 14:6).

Here Christ summarizes previous statements. He is the way to God; the only way to live. He is the truth about reality. He is the source and the center of life. He clearly states that He is the only means of access to God.

Jesus makes deliberate claims about Himself with a quiet sense of authority and finality. He does not add afterthoughts or revisions. He is not guessing, supposing or speaking with uncertainty.

Yet we should notice that these are not the self-giving claims of an egotist. Jesus always speaks for the benefit of the hearer. He is the Bread of life who gives life. He is the Light of the world who gives light. He is the Resurrection and the life who gives victory over death.

We should also notice that when men worshipped Christ and believed Him to be God, He did not correct them. He accepted and in fact *asked for* their total commitment to Him as God.

Two of the finest quotations I have ever read on this subject were written by C.S. Lewis:

> Then comes the real shock. Among these Jews there suddenly turns up a man who goes about talking as if He was God. He claims to forgive sins. He says He has always existed. He says He is coming to judge the world at the end of time. Now let us get this clear.
>
> Among the Pantheists anyone might say that he was a part of God, or one with God: there would be nothing very odd about it. But this man, since He was a Jew, would not mean that kind

30

of God. God, in their language, meant the Being outside the world who made it and was infinitely different from anything else. And when you have grasped that, you will see that what this man said was quite simply, the most shocking thing that has ever been uttered by human lips.

His second statement is more emphatic:

I'm ready to accept Jesus as a great moral teacher, but I don't accept His claim to be God. That is the one thing we must not say. A man who was merely a man and said the sort of things Jesus said would not be a great moral teacher. He would either be a lunatic—on a level with the man who says he is a poached egg—or else he would be the Devil of Hell. You must make your choice. Either this man was, and is, the Son of God; or else a madman or something worse. You can shut Him up for a fool, you can spit at Him and kill Him as a demon; or you can fall at His feet and call Him Lord and God. But let us not come with any patronizing nonsense about His being a great human teacher. He has not left that open to us. He did not intend to.

Dr. Philip Schaff, a church historian, underlines the fact that Jesus could not be anything less than He claimed to Be:

Is such an intellect—clear as the sky, bracing as the mountain air, sharp and penetrating as a sword, thoroughly healthy and vigorous, always ready and always self-possessed—liable to radical and most serious delusion concerning His own character and mission? Preposterous imagination!

31

CHRIST'S PERFECT CHARACTER

Kenneth Scott Latourette of Yale University said, "It is not His teachings which make Jesus so remarkable, although these would be enough to give Him distinction. It is a combination of the teachings with the man Himself. The two cannot be separated."

The life and character of Jesus Christ strongly reinforces my personal conviction that Christianity is true. I already explained why I believe that His words and the description of Him found in the Bible are reliable. Beyond that, His own life confirms His claims. As I study Jesus Christ, I must love and follow Him as a Christian.

What is Jesus remembered for in the Bible? For His selflessness, His integrity and His compassion. As He Himself said, "The Son of Man did not come to be served, but to serve, and give His life a ransom for many" (Mark 10:45).

How was He described as He traveled throughout the area in which He lived? "Jesus went through all the towns and villages, teaching in their synagogues, preaching the good news of the kingdom and healing every kind of disease and sickness. When He saw the crowds, He had compassion on them, because they were harassed and helpless, like sheep without a shepherd" (Matthew 9:35, 36).

Behind His magnetic personality stood His perfect sinlessness. This is important considering His claims to be God. It's critically important considering His crucifixion, where, as the sinless Savior, He would bear the penalty for our sins.

Three further quotations that stress Christ's character and sinlessness can be helpful to us in grasping the significance of who Christ was and what He came into the world to do.

Dr. Philip Schaff says:

> Such was Jesus of Nazareth—a true man in body, soul and spirit, yet differing from all men; a character unique and original from tender childhood to ripe manhood, moving in unbroken union with God, overflowing with love to man, free from every sin and error, innocent and holy, devoted to the noblest ends, teaching and practising all virtues in perfect harmony, sealing the purest life with the sublimest death.

John Stott says in *Basic Christianity:*

> This utter disregard for self in the service of God and man is what the Bible calls love. There is no self-interest in love. The essence of love is self-service. The worst of men is adorned by an occasional flash of such nobility, but the love of Jesus eradicated it with a never-fadding incandescent glow. Jesus was sinless because He was selfless.

Dr. Wilbur Smith, a preacher and writer I loved to hear speak, says:

> The outstanding characteristic of Jesus in His earthly life was the one in which all of us acknowledge we fall so short, and yet which at the same time all men recognize as the most priceless characteristic any man can have, namely, absolute goodness, or, to phrase it otherwise, perfect purity, genuine holiness, and in the case of Jesus, nothing less than sinlessness.

If a man of this caliber calls me to commitment, I am more than willing to follow Him and take His name as a Christian.

THE DEATH OF CHRIST

Central to Christianity is the death and resurrection of Jesus Christ. Each of the four gospels deals with the death and resurrection of Jesus, to the very details of His betrayal, His trial, the scene of His death, His last words and the words of those who saw Him when He arose again.

Christ came into our world with a purpose. He came to die as a sacrifice for our sins, to make us right with God.

When He was born it was announced, "You are to give Him the name Jesus, because He will save His people from their sins" (Matthew 1:21).

As He began to teach, He explained the nature of His mission: "For God so loved the world that He gave His one and only Son, that whoever believes in Him shall not perish but have eternal life" (John 3:16).

Before we can understand the Cross of Jesus Christ and why it was necessary for Him to die, we must understand something of our own human sinfulness.

The word "sin" is a difficult one. Used in the wrong way, or at the wrong time, it is an object of scorn. But properly understood, it reveals our basic human nature and its failings.

Sin is basically our human nature with its tendency to do what is wrong. We are born with this problem; we have it all our lives. Sin can be described as breaking God's laws or falling short of God's perfect standard. It can be described as our willful independence from the God who created us and loves us, although this independence may be just a quiet indifference rather than an active rebellion against God. Sin can be decribed in terms of results which each of us knows well.

The ultimate result of our sin is that it separates us from the God whom we were created to love and worship. Because we have been separated from Him, all these problems in the world and in our own lives arise. But because God loves us, He wants to bring us back into relationship with Himself, now and forever.

The only means possible by which the penalty of our sins can be sufficiently paid and our relationship with God restored is in Jesus Christ dying in our place. That is the heart of the Christian gospel. "God demonstrates His own love for us in this: While we were still sinners, Christ died for us" (Romans 5:8).

This matter of the death and resurrection of Christ is understood in many different ways. Sometimes it is explained in symbolic terms. At other times it is misunderstood as a tragic and sorrowful end to Jesus' life. Or we take it for granted, as if no response were necessary. Most often it is simply not thought about much. But interestingly, the fact of Jesus' death is not denied by many people.

Seldom, however, does the full impact of His death hit us. Here was Jesus of Nazareth, dying a *real* death, on a *real* cross, at a *real* place and time—for us. Such a sacrifice deserves and demands our response of repentance and sorrow for our sin and the request for forgiveness.

THE RESURRECTION OF CHRIST

As I remarked earlier, central to Christianity is the death and resurrection of Jesus Christ. Had He only died, His death would have been similar to the death of many great men. But He claimed power over death. His resurrection was necessary to prove this power.

The strength of the early Christian church was built on the confidence that Jesus had indeed risen again. The hope of all Christians is centered on the fact that

Jesus Christ rose again and is now alive—that He is indeed God and is the "resurrection and the life" that He claimed to be.

While many of us may waver on this fact of the resurrection, let us consider some of the evidence that leads to the conclusion that the resurrection is true.

The Bible states very clearly that Jesus arose from the dead. I already discussed the reliability and trustworthiness of the Bible on this point. In fact, the central theme of much of the New Testament is the resurrection of Christ.

Although Jesus was crucified publicly by official Roman executioners and then placed in a carefully guarded tomb, three days later that tomb was empty.

Various explanations for the empty tomb stretch the imagaination even more than the straightforward explanation recorded in the Bible. One explanation maintains that Jesus fainted on the cross but revived in the coolness of the tomb. But this does not take into account such factors as the expertise of the executioners, the extreme exhaustion had Jesus survived, the tight wrapping of the shroud, the heavy stone sealing the tomb, the Roman guards and the lack of any future appearances except in His resurrected form.

The stealing of Christ's body by His disciples is even harder to imagine because of the presence of the Roman guards. Nor is adequate explanation given for the powerful transformation in the lives of the disciples after their discovery that Jesus was alive again.

What could account for the power of the early church as it proclaimed the good news so fearlessly that Jesus had risen again, if He had not actually appeared to them? (Remember the disciples and the others had left the scene of the crucifixion disillusioned and helpless until they met the risen Christ.)

OUR FAITH TODAY

Where does the power of changed lives come from today if everything that Christians believe is based on a fraud? Why are so many lives beautifully and positively changed as they encounter the living Christ?

B.F. Westcott, a well-known theologian, writes:

> Indeed, taking all the evidence together, it is not too much to say that there is no historic incident better or more variously supported than the resurrection of Christ. Nothing but the antecedent assumption that it must be false would have suggested the idea of deficiency in the proof of it.

Henry Morris writes:

> The fact of His resurrection is the most important event of history and therefore, appropriately, is one of the most certain facts in all history.

OUR RESPONSE TO JESUS CHRIST

Our ultimate understanding of Jesus Christ lies in our own response to Him. This response is not a light matter. Jesus makes claims that are unique and exclusive. His death and resurrection are clear. But what still remains is our response to Him; in fact, He Himself calls for our response. When we finally see Christ as God and give Him the allegiance of our hearts and lives, then we will begin to see the total picture of His identity and mission. But not until then.

A friend of mine once said that we can examine the life of Jesus Christ as long as we want to, we can see His unique and persuasive attributes, we can be awed by His death and resurrection, but until we humbly accept Him as our Lord, we still fail to adequately understand Him. Only when we accept Him as Savior and properly place Him as Lord of our lives, do we begin to fully understand who He is. Only then will we see Christ as the Son of God and the Savior of the world.

Dr. John Stott, while speaking to a group of students at the University of Michigan about Jesus Christ, concluded:

> *I want to end in my last minute on a practical note. If the basic Christian thesis is true, and Jesus is the Son of God, then you can never be the same after your discovery as you were before. You cannot fit Jesus at the end of a microscope or at the end of a telescope and say, "How interesting!" Jesus Christ is not interesting. He is profoundly morally and spiritually disturbing and challenging. If there is anybody who forces us to get off the fence and to enter the field of moral commitment, it is Jesus Christ. If He is God, He deserves our worship, not just our patronage. Not just our admiration but our adoration. It is my earnest prayer that many on this campus this week may come to find a true and sincere conviction that Jesus is the Son of God and may bring to Him the worship of their lives and of their hearts.*

4
The Evidence of Changed Lives

"We have missed the full impact of the Gospel if we have not discovered what it is to be ourselves, loved by God, irreplaceable in his sight, unique among our fellow men."
—Bruce Larson.

"Having sought for so long the real meaning and key to life, and having found it in Christ, I couldn't keep quiet about this discovery. Everybody had to know."—Geoffrey Shaw.

The third main reason that I am a Christian is because of the effect the Christian gospel has had in the changed lives of so many people throughout history and in the changed lives of so many people I know, including myself and my wife, Joan.

Perhaps this is one of the most convincing reasons why I am a Christian. The promises of God are proven true in personal experience. It is one thing to have a well-reasoned case for the validity of Christianity, but is is another thing to have the case proved right in front of our eyes.

The Christian gospel is more than an academic philosophy of life. It is more than a series of explanations of what God is like and why things are the way they are.

The word "gospel" means "good news"—the good news which announces that a person's life can be changed by the power of loving God.

Saint Paul changed from a persecutor of Christians into one of the greatest Christian leaders of all time. He said, "I am not ashamed of the gospel, because it is the power of God for the salvation of everyone who believes" (Romans 1:16). He also said, "If anyone is in Christ, he is a new creation; the old has gone, the new has come" (2 Corinthians 5:17).

Billy Graham has expressed this change so very well. "When you come to Christ, the Holy Spirit takes up residence in your heart. Something new is added to your life supernaturally. You are transformed by the renewing of your mind. A new power, a new dimension, a new ability to love, a new joy, a new peace—the Holy Spirit comes in and lives the Christian life through you."

The changes brought by the gospel touch the very core of our lives. The changes are powerful and positive. Hate is changed into love. Emptiness is filled with purpose and meaning. Unrest and anxiety are replaced by peace and trust in God. Selfishness is transformed into selflessness. Guilt finds forgiveness.

But most significantly, the destiny of a person who becomes a Christian is changed forever. He or she now becomes born again into a life that will never end. He or she has been given eternal life. This eternal life as Jesus referred to it has both a new *qualtity*—the quality of God's life—and a new *quantity*, which will never end, but will be eternal with God forever.

These changes are so profound that the mind boggles. What could ever produce such changes, even those we can observe, to say nothing of the deeper realities of forgiveness before God and eternal life with Him? I believe that only the God who made us can cause such things to happen.

Such changes are much more than a mere change of mind, a turning over of a new leaf, a psychological uplift or the power of positive thinking. They cannot be explained by charges of mass delusion. These changes are deep and real. The entire direction and quality of a person's life is forever changed. The greatest of all miracles takes place when one becomes a Christian. The fact that God comes into a life is the only reasonable explanation.

ENCOURAGING TESTIMONIES

Throughout history there have been remarkable stories of Christian conversion. One of the most dramatic stories is that of Saint Paul, who persecuted the early church. He met God in such a powerful way on the road to Damascus that he was converted—literally turned around from his pursuit of Christians to the pursuit of God! As he preached for the rest of his life, he referred to his own conversion story as evidence of the truth and reality of the gospel.

The conversion of Saint Augustine, one of the world's greatest thinkers, is also one of the famous conversions in the early church. He records his conversion in his well-known book, *The Confessions of St. Augustine.*

John Newton, a slaving-ship captain in the 1700's said of his conversion: "I went to Africa that I might be able to sin to my heart's content. I was a wild beast on the coast of Africa till the Lord caught and tamed me." He later wrote hundreds of Christian hymns, including his well-known "Amazing Grace":

> *Amazing grace, how sweet the sound*
> *That saved a wretch like me!*
> *I once was lost, but now am found;*
> *Was blind, but now I see.*
>
> *'Twas grace that taught my heart to fear,*
> *And grace my fears relieved;*
> *How precious did that grace appear*
> *The hour I first believed.*
>
> *Thro' many dangers, toils and snares*
> *I have already come;*
> *'Tis grace that brought me safe thus far,*
> *And grace will lead me home.*
>
> *When we've been there ten thousand years,*
> *Bright shining as the sun,*
> *We've no less days to sing God's praise*
> *Than when we've first begun.*

Malcolm Muggeridge, a well-known British journalist, recently wrote the story of his own Christian conversion in *Jesus Rediscovered*.

Three well-worded quotations from that book show the validity and applicability of the gospel today by one of the greatest minds of our time:

> [This book] represents the efforts of one aging twentieth-century mind to give expression to a deep dissatisfaction with prevailing twentieth-century values and assumptions and a sense that there is an alternative—an alternative propounded two thousand years ago by the Sea of Galilee and on the hill called Golgotha.

He continues, speaking of the letters he receives:

> They reveal, I think more fully than any public opinion or other so-called scientific investigation, the extraordinary spiritual hunger which prevails today among all classes and conditions of people, from the most illiterate to the most educated, from the most lowly to the most eminent . . . The only means of satisfying it remains that bread of life which Jesus offered, with the promise that those who ate of it should never hunger again. The promise stands.

Finally Muggeridge says of becoming a Christian:

> So I come back to where I began, to that other King, one Jesus; to the Christian notion that man's efforts to make himself personally and collectively happy in earthly terms are doomed to failure. He must indeed as Christ said, be born again, be a new man, or he's nothing. So

at least I have concluded, have failed to find in past experience, present dilemma and future expectations, any alternative proposition. As far as I am concerned, it is Christ or nothing.

Likewise, Peter Marshall, Chaplain to the United States Senate, and upon whom the film "A Man Called Peter" was based, expresses his confidence in God's forgiveness in this way: "I think I may have to go through the agony of hearing all my sins recited in the presence of God. But I believe it will be like this—Jesus will come over and lay his hand across my shoulders and say to God, 'Yes, all these things are true, but I'm here to cover up for Peter. He is sorry for all his sins, and by a transaction made between us, I am now solely responsible for them.' "

The list of conversions and statements of faith of people is inexhaustible. Sports figures, entertainers, and politicians often lead the list of Christian stories, but only because they are more well known. Many thousands, even millions, of people can recount the story of how Jesus Christ has changed their lives.

As I travel throughout North America as well as other parts of the world and meet people of all ages and backgrounds, I am amazed and thrilled at the same story of change and joy that God accomplishes in each different life. I am reminded of the statement by Elton Trueblood, who said, "The ultimate verification of our religion consists of the changed lives to which it can point and for which it is responsible."

The power which God brings into a life is so full and complete that it includes amazing responses to crises of life. I know of countless stories and have met many people who have proved the reality of Christianity in their personal lives.

Corrie ten Boom, a Dutch Christian, offered refuge

to Jewish people during World War II. She was eventually imprisoned and saw her sister die in a concentration camp. Her faith in God during such suffering is one of the great Christian stories today. I have heard her speak. The love and joy that radiates from this woman cannot be explained apart from the reality of the gospel.

Helmut Thielicke, a German pastor-theologian who preached the love of God in war-torn Germany to crowds of thousands, did not speak of an empty faith. Thielicke spoke of a God who is so real and so concerned that He knows our every heartbreak, our every sorrow. He said, "We walk beneath an open heaven and we know who watches over us and if we fall we know into whose hands we will fall."

Recently we had Joni Eareckson, author of the books *Joni* and *A Step Further* on our television program. She is a quadriplegic as a result of a diving accident several years ago. She is also one of the most vibrant and thoughtful people I have ever met.

With clear and confident statements she expressed her love for her Savior and her absolute confidence that "all things work together for good to those who love God" (Romans 8:28). She said she praises God not in spite of her wheelchair but because of it. Before she had had only slight thoughts of God. Now she knows Him so much more and her life is so much richer.

If you have never read her two books I would urge you to immediately do so. Here is real Christianity at work in a human life.

As an ancient Christian said to an ancient king "If you accept this Gospel and become Christ's man, you will stumble on wonder upon wonder and every wonder true."

These are not isolated instances. It is the common

response of those who have experienced the reality of knowing God.

THE FINAL TEST

Perhaps the final test of Christian reality is in the face of death, an inevitable crisis for all of us. Christians are prepared in the fullest sense of the word to die.

Recently I attended the funeral of a young couple, Jim and Susan, who were engaged to be married in a month. They had been tragically killed in an automobile accident.

They had been very active as Christians and knew many people. The church was crowded and both families filled several pews. While there was genuine sorrow over their deaths, there was also a genuine trust in God and confidence in the life beyond the grave. The funeral was one of faith in the promises of God as Jim's brother and sister sang a Christian song. The entire service was moving as we faced the realities of life and death with the greater reality of Jesus Christ and His promise of everlasting life.

One young man who took part in the funeral told me afterwards that he could see the joy in the faces of the two families as Scriptures were read and songs were sung. That to me is overwhelming evidence that the gospel is true, and is able to satisfy fully that "longing within," even beyond the grave.

5

The Importance
Of Your Decision

"Beware of letting slip this note of decisiveness, this belief in the definite nature of the passing from "not being a disciple" to "being a disciple" from being "out of Christ," "away," "lost" to being "in Christ," "home," and "found.""

—Canon Bryan Green

"To be a Christian means to have a vital, personal relationship with Jesus Christ. Until that is established all other concerns are secondary."

—L. Nelson Bell.

I have tried to explain why I became a Christian and why I am convinced that being a Christian satisfied this "longing within."

C.S. Lewis said, "Christianity, if false, is of no importance, and if true, of infinite importance. The one thing it cannot be is moderately important." Being a Christian is important to me because the gospel deals with my life all of my life and because it deals with my eternal life in the world to come.

THE NEED FOR A REAL GOSPEL

It is no accident that the gospel relates to our everyday lives. We were created in the image of God; that means we have a capacity to know Him and to be in a vital relationship with Him. But this capacity has not been exercised and so our relationship with God has been tragically broken.

We live our lives, for the most part, on our own, independent of God. Yet our lives are not rich and full and meaningful. Somehow they are not complete. We are not truly happy, but we don't know why. There is an emptiness and a longing for something more.

Jesus said, "A man's life does not consist in the abundance of his possessions" (Matthew 4:4).

What do these often-quoted verses really mean? We know we are more than physical beings. We have a spiritual dimension that cannot exist without being in relationship to God or depending on His Word in the Bible. We have forgotten our Creator and instead fallen in love with His creation. And our lives are the poorer for it.

I find it significant that Jesus in the New Testament uses the familiar word "Father" for God. The Lord's Prayer begins, "Our Father in heaven, hallowed be your name . . . " In the famous Sermon the Mount (Matthew 5-7) Jesus speaks of God as "Father" or "heavenly Father" no less than 14 times. This tells us a great deal about the nature of a loving God, but it also tells us about the relationship we ought to have with Him. He ought to be the Father whom we trust.

The first of the Ten Commandments begins, "I am the Lord your God . . . you shall have no other gods before Me" (Exodus 20:2, 3). When Jesus was asked to name the great commandments, He summarized the relationship we are supposed to have with God by saying, Love the Lord your God with all your heart, and with all your soul and with all your mind. This is the first and greatest commandment" (Matthew 22:37, 38).

Dethroning God from His proper place is actually the breaking of this commandment; this is the greatest sin we commit. Dr. Roy Bell of First Baptist Church in Vancouver defines sin as "self-destructive behavior." That is precisely what we do when we tune God out of the picture of our lives. We literally destroy ourselves. We make ourselves less than what we were intended to be. We need only to read the newspapers and look into the faces and lives of people around us to know that this is true.

Anything built on a shaky foundation threatens to ultimately collapse. When we try to build our lives without God, we are doomed to failure.

History is the history of war. International relationships are fraught with problems. National issues only intensify problems within society. Marriage and family problems occur in everyone's life. And we all share feelings of loneliness, depression, guilt and fear.

OUR LIVES IN THIS WORLD

Does the gospel have anything to say about our lives in this world? Yes! A thousand times yes! The purpose for Jesus Christ coming into this world was to bring us back into a relationship with God. "God was in Christ reconciling [bringing back together] the world to Himself" (2 Corinthians 5:19 RSV).

When we come back to God and build our lives in trust and dependence on Him, we build a solid foundation. This is not as easy as it sounds. We need to diligently apply ourselves to a loving God with all our hearts, souls and minds. As one young friend said to me, "I don't want easy answers, but I want right answers."

This new life starts with a single step. It begins when we come back to God and become reunited with Him in Jesus Christ. In fact, that's what "Christian" means—to be "in Christ." A Christian is someone who accepts Christ as the significant Person in his life. He has given himself to God and can talk to God as his Father and to Jesus as his Lord. We will stumble and fall, but the Bible is our guidebook and the Holy Spirit is our Teacher and our source of strength.

As this new life grows, we can see results. Just as fruit on a tree indicates the kind of tree it really is, so Christians produce fruit which indicates the new nature they possess. The Bible even calls these characteristics the "fruit of the Spirit." "The fruit of the Spirit is love, joy, peace, patience, kindness, goodness, faithfulness, gentleness and self-control" (Galatians 5:22, 23).

As our new inner character is strengthened, so is our sense of purpose and meaning in life. Human relationships are affected and lives are changed. In fact, the world has been deeply affected and continues to be, by those Christians who have learned to practice the second of Jesus' great commandments to "love your neighbor as yourself" (Matthew 22:39).

Life as a Christian can be full and exciting. Two books that I recommend are written by Dr. Samuel Shoemaker and are titled *Extraordinary Living for Ordinary Men* and *The Adventure of Living Under New Management*. The titles tell the tale.

HEAVEN

We are too limited in our vision to understand what heaven will be like. But the most trusted Man who ever lived is the one who spoke most frequently about it. In one of the most beautiful pictures Jesus painted, He said:

> In my Father's house are many rooms; if it were not so, I would have told you. I am going there to prepare a place for you. And if I go and prepare a place for you, I will come back and take you to be with me, that you also may be where I am (John 14:2, 3).

Heaven is a permanent dwelling in God's house for all those who belong to Him.

There are many other pictures of heaven in the Bible. It is called the "City of God" where harmony and happiness reign:

> Then I saw a new heaven and a new earth, for the first heaven and the first earth had passed away, and there was no longer any sea. I saw the Holy City, the new Jerusalem, coming down out of heaven from God, prepared as a bride beautifully dressed for her husband. And I heard a loud voice from the throne saying, "Now the dwelling of God is with men and He will live with them." They will be His people and God Himself will be with them and be their God. He will wipe every tear from their eyes. There will be no more death or mourning or crying or pain, for the old order of things has passed away" (Revelation 21: 1-5).

See how this stresses the intent of the first commandment: we are restored to a relationship with God that fully satisfies our longing within.

The beginning of heaven is described as a "marriage supper" and can be understood like the experiences of joy and happiness that we witness at happy weddings.

Of all the many words and pictures of heaven recorded in the Bible, perhaps the most accurate one is "eternal" or "everlasting" life that has its source in God and will never end. "For God so loved the world that He gave His one and only Son, that whoever believes in Him shall not perish but have eternal life" (John 3:16).

Our prettiest pictures of heaven still fail to describe it fully. God, the Architect and the Creator of life in this world, is also the Architect and Creator of life in the world to come. We will find not only joy, but the source of joy. We will find not only love, the the One who first loved us! We will taste and experience reality as we have never fully known it before. We will be with God forever!

In a private letter to a friend, C.S. Lewis wrote:

> Think of yourself wintering in the earth: waiting to come up a flower in the Gardener's good time, up into the real world, the real waking. I suppose that our whole present life, looked back on from there will seem only a drowsy half-waking. We are here in the land of dreams. But cock-crow is coming. It is nearer than when I began this letter.

HELL

Hell is a very difficult subject to talk about, partly because it is so often distorted and partly because it is such a horrible reality.

Jesus spoke about hell. He so adamantly warned us to avoid it at all costs that He gave His life to save us from it.

Dwight L. Moody, the evangelist known as the preacher of love, once said, "When we preach on hell, we might at least do it with tears in our eyes."

Hell is not to be dismissed lightly. It is the permanent existence of those who have chosen to live without God. Since love and joy and peace find their source in God, hell will be the absence of all that is good and beautiful, because God will not be there. Hell is everlasting separation from the presence of God. It is the result of an irreversible decision. Jesus warned us to flee from hell. He used the strongest words possible to describe the torment and the agony of those who fall into it. Dante in his *Inferno* wrote over the gate of hell, "All hope abandon, ye who enter here."

Hell is an extension of the choice to live without God. We make our own decision to enter it, but I am not sure

we face up to its reality. Otherwise we would heed
Jesus' words and choose to turn to Him and receive His
gift of eternal life.

Evangelist Billy Graham had this insight into hell:

> Hell is not prepared for man. God never meant
> that man would ever go to hell. Hell was
> prepared for the devil and his angels, but man
> rebelled against God and followed the devil . . .
> Hell is essentially and basically banishment
> from the presence of God for deliberately rejec-
> ting Jesus Christ as Lord and Savior.

Hell will be the unavoidable destiny of those at God's
final judgment who will not receive mercy. It will be the
result of our own choice. No one will be unfairly judg-
ed. Let me urge you to weigh the cost of rejecting the
gift of eternal life made by Jesus Christ.

6

How to Become a Christian

"The Publican stood afar off and beat his breast and said 'Lord, be merciful to me, a sinner.' I tell you that man had the finest theology of any man in all England."—Charles Spurgeon.

"If you have never heard the mountains singing, or seen the trees of the field clapping their hands, do not think because of that that they don't. Ask God to open your ears so you may hear it, and your eyes so you may see it, because, though few men ever know it, they do, my friend, they do."—McCandlish Phillips.

"There are two things to do about the gospel—believe it and behave it."
—Susannah Wesley.

The greatest decision you can make in your life is to become a Christian. It is no small decision. It will change the course of your life right now, and it will change your life forever.

Yet it is amazing how few people know what it really means to become a Christian. Surveys indicate that almost 90 percent of the population cannot give a clear definition of what a Christian is or how to become one.

I remember a conversation I had on an airplane not too long ago with a young woman enrolled in graduate studies. After we talked about her courses, I asked her if she could comment on a question I often asked. Could she tell me what a Christian was? She started to reply, but then stopped. "When you first asked the question, I thought I knew the answer," she said. "But then I realized I didn't." The idea of being a Christian seems so commonplace and the word is used so often that she thought she knew. But after thinking about it, she realized she could not give any answer at all.

This is not an isolated instance. As I talk with hundreds of people, I find that the vast majority have very little understanding of what Christianity is. Yet most people become interested when they begin to understand what it means to become a Christian in the sense of personally following Jesus Christ.

I am convinced that one of our biggest problems in discussing Christianity today is communication. People aren't rejecting true Christianity so much as a false image of Christianity. They either have the wrong idea of what Christianity is, or, more specifically, little idea of genuine Christianity.

BECOMING A CHRISTIAN

So how do you become a Christian? First, let me make a distinction. *Becoming* a Christian is one matter. *Living* as a Christian is another. Pointing out the difference will help explain what it means to become a Christian at all.

Many people have an idea that you are a "Christian" if you live a good life, "a Christian life." It is something that does not have a clear beginning or a specific content. The term is almost an automatic reward for achieving a certain level of goodness—and the level varies to fit the situation.

This assumption misses the point in two ways: the Christian life is not a matter of your own goodness, but a life lived by the love and power of God with specific content to it. Even more seriously, it demands a personal response from us.

In other words, you don't live like a Christian to become one. You must first establish a personal relationship with God. Then you continue to live within that relationship. There has to be a beginning when a very miraculous event takes place in your life and you are born into the family of God.

MAKING A DECISION

There must be a personal response to God's love, a

personal entrance into a relationship with God. This is another way of saying that the experience must be real to you. This needs to be emphasized, for often Christianity is taken for granted. We live in a "Christian" country. We come from "Christian" homes. We belong to "Christian" churches. We may even recite "Christian" prayers. But we may never have taken to heart the matter of our own personal relationship with God through Christ.

There is a decisiveness in your becoming a Christian, a clarity of undersanding that provokes a genuine response in your heart and mind and will when you decide to take Jesus Christ seriously and to begin a new way of life.

In a thousand different ways, God can speak into a thousand different lives, and we can respond to Him. Some of us respond slowly, some more quickly. Some of us struggle mightily, while others take that step almost immediately. Yet each person is drawn toward God by the quiet persuasion of the Holy Spirit. The concept of becoming a Christian becomes clear. The desire grows. The search for God intensifies us to the one Savior, Jesus Christ, to commit our lives to Him. The story is basically the same in each life: the emphasis is always on the goodness and love of God. God can speak to us through the Bible, through people, through events and even through our thoughts.

THE NEW BIRTH

Perhaps the best example of becoming a Christian is the one used by Jesus Christ as He spoke to a religious leader named Nicodemus. He said, "I tell you the truth, unless a man is born again, he cannot see the kingdom of God" (John 3:3).

The words "born again" literally mean "born from above" or born of God." Jesus explained to the puzzled Nicodemus, "I tell you the truth, unless a man is born of water and the Spirit, he cannot enter the kingdom of God. Flesh gives birth to flesh, but the Spirit gives birth to spirit" (John 3:5-6). As physical birth leads to physical life, our spiritual birth leads to spiritual life.

This, then, is where we begin. This is how we become Christians, by being "born again" spiritually by the power of God. Only God can bring about this new birth, which is actually a miraculous action of God in the human heart and life. It is a birth into a new dimension of life we didn't even know existed before. It is the entrance into God's life that begins now and will never end.

The term "born again" has received tremendous attention in the past few years. Because of some over-reaction to the phrase, I often use the term "born anew" to communicate this central Christian concept. Regardless of the actual words the concept is all important. As we have seen, it actually began with Jesus Christ and it has been used by Christians throughout the ages to communicate the idea of becoming a Christian.

George Whitfield, an eighteenth-century Christian speaker, wrote to Benjamin Franklin:

> As you have made a pretty considerable pro-
> gress in the mysteries of electricity, I would now
> honestly recommend to your diligent unpre-
> judiced pursuit and study the mysteries of
> the new birth.

To be "born anew" means to become a child of God in the full sense of the term. Only then can we say with confidence "Our Father in heaven" in the relationship of a child to the heavenly Father. Christianity as a relationship with God gives us a new birth into a new family—the family of God. The Bible says:

> Yet to all who received Him, to those who believed in His name, He gave the right to become children of God—children born not of natural descent, nor of human decision or a husband's will, but born of God (John 1:12, 13).

REPENTANCE

There are three stages in becoming a Christian: repentance, faith and the new birth. We do the first two and God then does the third, although it is actually God who helps us and even causes us to accomplish the first two.

Repentance is the sincere and radical change of our heart or mind that demands a "turning away" from one thing and a "turning to" another. It means being sorry for our sins and turning to God for His forgiveness.

A large part of repentance is triggered by the growing awareness of our need for repentance. This takes place as we become conscious of our sinfulness. We have not only committed more sins than we could ever number or remember, but we also have sinful human hearts. Our human nature is thoroughly tainted by this sinfulness. Sin is the tendency to live our lives independently of God, leaving Him out of the picture and allowing all wrong actions and shortcomings to happen.

There are three basic words in the Bible for sin: transgression, which means to step over the line or to break the laws of God; iniquity, which means to do what is wrong; and sin, which means to miss the mark or to fall short of God's standards.

59

"Conviction" is the word often used to describe the growing sense of our sinfulness and the guilt which we bring upon ourselves in the eyes of a holy God. As we begin to be sorry and to repent of our sins this is the result of the Holy Spirit convicting us.

Repentance is taking our sinfulness seriously enough to take definite action. It leads us to confession before God and to the sincere request for His forgiveness. In fact, the word for "confession" means "to agree with God concerning our sins."

Listen to the words of King David when he was convicted of his sinfulness before God:

> Have mercy on me, O God;
> according to thy abundant mercy blot out my
>   transgressions.
> Wash me thoroughly from iniquity, and
> cleanse me
>   from my sin.
> For I know my transgressions and my sin is
> ever
>   before me.
> Against thee, thee only, have I sinned,
> and done that which is evil in thy sight,
> so that thou art justified in they sentence and
> blameless
>   in thy judgment (Psalm 51:1-4 KJV alt).

Emil Brunner, a well-known theologian, says this about repentance:

> Repentance is the despair of self, despairing of
> self-help in removing the guilt that we have
> brought upon us. Repentance means a radical
> turning away from self-reliance to trust in God
> alone. To repent means to recognize self-trust
> to be the heart of sin.

And Martin Luther adds, "To do so no more is the truest repentance."

Have you ever confessed your sins to God, repenting of your sinfulness and acknowledging your need of

Him? If you never have, this is the first step to being born again.

FAITH

The second step after repentance is faith. Faith is believing what God has said and done in His dealings with us. It is placing our trust in Him, turning to Him and to His promise of forgiveness after we have turned from our sinfulness.

Faith is a misunderstood concept. It is not a blind leap into the ark, or a belief in something against all the evidence. To the contrary, faith is the growing conviction that something is true because of the mounting evidence.

I repeat the definition of faith I gave earlier. "Faith is the resting of the mind on the sufficiency of the evidence." There are two parts to this statement. Faith is both the result of a growing confidence that something is true and the desire to do something because of that growing confidence. We can rest our minds upon it.

Trust is perhaps the best word to convey the idea of faith in God. To trust means that we not only believe that what someone has said is true, but we are willing to act as well. And we are able to trust Jesus Christ with our lives much more confidently than we do with other people.

To have faith in God or to trust our lives to Jesus Christ means to believe that Jesus will forgive our sins and give us eternal life as He promised He would—if we ask Him.

COMMITTING YOUR LIFE

"Behold, I stand at the door and knock," Christ says.

"If anyone hears my voice and opens the door, I will come in" (Revelation 3:20 KJV alt.).

Jesus Christ is speaking of what it means to ask Him into our lives and to trust Him. As we hear Him knocking and invite Him in, He comes in just as He promised.

Someone once said, "Becoming a Christian is when we stop saying 'please' to God and begin saying 'thank you'." A "please" must be said only once, and when the answer is given we do not need to ask again. We can now begin saying "thank you" and we can say it the rest of our lives. Worship is actually the deep and full expression of saying "thank you" to God for who He is and what He has done.

Have you ever experienced the miracle of the new birth? Have you ever become aware that you need God? Have you ever prayed to receive Christ into your life?

I cannot stress enough the urgency of making that decision. The question is not whether you should repent, but when: now.

As C.S. Lewis said:

> When the author walks onto the stage the play is over. God is going to invade, all right: but what is the good of saying you are on His side then, when you see the whole natural universe melting away like a dream . . . like a dream and something else—something it never entered your head to conceive comes crashing in . . . that will not be the time for choosing: it will be the time when we discover which side we really have chosen, whether we realized it before or not. Now, today, this moment, is our chance to choose the right side.

LIVING AS A CHRISTIAN

After you become a Christian, you need to develop your new Christian life. Take it seriously; look for every source of help you can find. Five suggestions might help:

* *Find a good church that clearly presents Jesus Christ as Savior and Lord.
* *Find some good Christian friends with whom you can talk, pray and study the Bible.
* *Begin the daily habit of reading the Bible. Use a study guide or at least read one chapter a day, quietly and thoughtfully, allowing God to speak to you through it. Start with the Gospel of Matthew and use a bookmark as you work through the New Testament. Then tackle the Old Testament.
* *Begin the daily habit of prayer. Talk to God as if He were there and listening—for He is. Pray in thanksgiving for what He has done and in request for specific areas in which you need His help. And begin to pray for others.
* *Begin sharing Jesus Christ. The same Lord who loves you loves others, too. You can be the channel through which He reaches into many other lives. This will serve to strengthen you and bring joy into your life.

YOUR DECISION

Deciding to follow Jesus Christ is the most important decision you will ever make. Much leads up to this decision, but the time comes when you must decide. If you believe that you now have weighed the evidence and are convinced the gospel is true, may I urge you to make the decision to become a Christian now. Postponed decisions have a way of never being made.

There are two main areas in our response to God's invitation to trust Him. First, we need to repent of our sins, confessing them to God and asking for His forgiveness. Then, we need to personally invite Jesus Christ into our lives, having faith or confidence that He will come in as He promised to do if we ask Him. As we respond in this twofold way, He beautifully and miraculously hears our thoughts and prayers and enters into our lives at that very moment of time.

Here is a simple prayer that I suggest you make:

> *Dear God, I confess my sins to you. I repent of them and will turn from them as you help me. Thank you for sending Jesus Christ to die upon the cross for me. Now please come into my heart and life and forgive me and establish your presence within me, causing me to be born again. Thank you for hearing my prayer and for answering it. Please give me the confidence that you have heard and answered my prayer and give me the strength to grow as a new Christian. In Jesus' name. Amen.*

If you have honestly prayed that prayer—congratulations! It is your first and all-important prayer as a new Christian.

POSTSCRIPT

If you have just embarked on your new journey of faith I would like to encourage you.

Discover all you can, in every way, about your new faith. Find other Christians and share your experiences and thoughts together. There may be times of discouragement and doubt, but on the other side of the clouds the sun is still shining. Learn to depend on the trustworthiness of the Bible and of Jesus Christ, and not on your feelings. It is the Christian gospel we need to count on. The evidence for its credibility and reliability is more than sufficient.

> *And this is the testimony: God has given us eternal life, and this life is in his Son. He who has the Son has life; he who does not have the Son of God does not have life. I write these things to you who believe in the name of the Son of God so that you may know that you have eternal life.*
> *(I John 5:11-13).*